W9-AUD-458

50 BOSSES

WORSE THAN YOURS

BY THE SAME AUTHOR

50 Jobs Worse Than Yours
50 Relatives Worse Than Yours
50 Boyfriends Worse Than Yours
50 Days Worse Than Yours
50 Dates Worse Than Yours
J. Crewd

50

BOSSES

WORSE
THAN
YOURS

Justin Racz

BLOOMSBURY

Copyright © 2007 by Justin Racz

All rights reserved. No part of this book may be used or reproduced in any manner whatsoever without written permission from the publisher except in the case of brief quotations embodied in critical articles or reviews. For information address Bloomsbury USA, 175 Fifth Avenue, New York, NY 10010.

Published by Bloomsbury USA, New York
Distributed to the trade by Holtzbrinck Publishers

All papers used by Bloomsbury USA are natural, recyclable products made from wood grown in well-managed forests. The manufacturing processes conform to the environmental regulations of the country of origin.

LIBRARY OF CONGRESS CATALOGING-IN-PUBLICATION DATA HAS BEEN APPLIED FOR.

ISBN-10 1-59691-324-X
ISBN-13 978-1-59691-324-0

First U.S. Edition 2007

1 3 5 7 9 10 8 6 4 2

Designed and typeset by Elizabeth Van Itallie
Printed in Singapore by Tien Wah Press

To my former bosses who encouraged me to be self-employed

Bosses

1. The Former Thespian
2. The Big-Game Hunter
3. The Napoleon
4. The Veteran
5. The Former All-American
6. The Made Man
7. First Position of Power
8. The Heir Apparent
9. The M.B.A.
10. Chief Elusive Officer
11. Big Brother
12. The Psychopath
13. The Chair Chucker
14. Talk to the Hand
15. The Progressive
16. The Pimp
17. By-the-Book Betty
18. The Jokester
19. Wants to Be Your Buddy
20. The Letch
21. The Whiz Kid
22. The Micromanager
23. Pregnant Boss
24. Balding Boss

25. The Twelve-Stepper
26. Mr. Hollywood
27. The Sleigh Driver
28. The Memo-ist
29. The Patriarch
30. 30-Across
31. Recently Separated
32. Tenured
33. The Dilettante
34. The Misanthrope
35. The Backstabber
36. The Junior Capitalist
37. Mr. Clean
38. The Dropout
39. Pharaoh
40. Madame Secretary
41. Hot Boss (B.I.L.F.)
42. The Blue Blood
43. The Screamer
44. Mr. Wonderful
45. Mr. Five-Point Plan
46. The Infirm
47. Out to Pasture
48. The Fitness Fanatic
49. The Ventriloquist
50. '70s Dude Turned Corporate
51. Your Boss

1. The Former Thespian

THE BOSS

During meetings he brags about his role as Hamlet in summer stock. So far, he has yet to take any sort of lead at the company. Everyone knows he takes off early to audition for commercials, mostly voice-over work—the fast-talking legal guy at the end of the spot.

DANGER

Company karaoke outing at Singnatures.

HE SAID

"The theater critic at the *Saratoga Gazette* said, and I quote, 'Never have I seen, nor will I again, such a modern interpretation of Hamlet. Who knew Elsinore was in Brooklyn?'"

BENEFIT

Found his Best Actor acceptance speech.

DRAWBACK

He refers to you as his understudy.

HOW TO DEAL

Run lines with him for the part of Jean Valjean in a touring company.

2. The Big-Game Hunter

THE BOSS

During the week, he's a criminal defense attorney as well your mentor, selected by your law firm. On weekends, he antiques at the country gun shop. He insists you include photos of his latest kills in PowerPoint presentations. And the company picnic—paintball with high-powered assault rifles—is no picnic.

WARDROBE

Camouflage iPod nano skin.

DÉCOR

Bearskin rug. Yes, with head.

BENEFIT

The baby-seal-lined gloves he gave you for Christmas.

DRAWBACK

He signed you up on the NRA mailing list.

HOW TO DEAL

Tell him the second amendment is your favorite, too.

3. The Napoleon

THE BOSS

Intent on world domination, but can't see over his desk.

WARDROBE

Platform shoes.

DÉCOR

A footstool for you.

BENEFIT

He can't see when you roll your eyes.

DRAWBACK

Takes advantage of his height by asking the skirted interns to grab things from the top shelf for him.

HOW TO DEAL

Make him feel dominant: Remain seated.

4. The Veteran

THE BOSS

Honorably discharged and still in search of something to command. He tells you more about shrapnel and "Charlie" than you want to know, but he can't remember all those times when you covered for him and saved his butt.

HE SAID

"Meet me in the conference room at 0900 hours. Get there late and you're on latrine detail, Johnson."

BENEFIT

He does more before six a.m. than most people do all day.

DRAWBACK

One-arm push-up contests.

BONUS

Code reds.

HOW TO DEAL

Move to the Canada branch.

5. The Former
All-American

THE BOSS

Led the conference in pass completion percentage, but blew out his knee in the championship. He got red-shirted during college, missed the draft, and is now your superior.

WARDROBE

Varsity jacket.

HE SAID

"For tomorrow's meeting, I want everyone to bring their A game."

BENEFIT

Your company football team is undefeated.

DRAWBACK

The morning "huddle."

HOW TO DEAL

Score brownie points by asking to see that "Where Are They Now" article from *Sports Illustrated*.

6. The Made Man

THE BOSS

He doesn't give health benefits, but your money's tax free.

INCIDENT

He makes you start his car.

HE SAID

"Do me this favor. I won't forget it."

BENEFIT

He knows a guy who knows a guy.

DRAWBACK

You can never quit.

HOW TO DEAL

Rat him out and cop a plea.

7. First Position of Power

THE BOSS

She's answered too many phones to let up now.

WARDROBE

Power suit. Tight bun. Gym bag.

DÉCOR

Aeron chair, the chair that says "I've made it."

BENEFIT

Tell her what your co-workers said about her and she'll spare you on your next review.

DRAWBACK

Tell your co-workers what she said about them and you're fired.

HOW TO DEAL

Tell her she looks thin.

8. The Heir Apparent

THE BOSS

Barely graduated and never worked a day in his life, but is now being groomed to take over his father's company.

WARDROBE

Ketchup-stained tie, wrinkled khakis, tube socks.

HE SAID

"This is what I call a BORED meeting!!"

BENEFIT

Four-hour beer-and-buffet lunches at McLaughlin's.

DRAWBACK

They can't fire him, but they can fire you.

HOW TO DEAL

Marry into the family.

9. The M.B.A.

THE BOSS

Well paid, overeducated, speaks in acronyms—B2Bs, WSJ, FT, HBS—because he has no time to waste. Basically, he's an Excel and PowerPoint jockey with a license to manage.

WARDROBE

Hair gel, Gordon Gekko style.

HE SAID

"Um, I don't do toner."

BENEFIT

If you're nice to him, he'll do your taxes for you.

DRAWBACK

He gets testy if you touch his laptop.

HOW TO DEAL

Join his fantasy football league.

10. Chief Elusive Officer

THE BOSS

Stock market guru, fast talker, option backdater, prisoner #078025.

WARDROBE

Armani. This is the standard minimum-security-prison suit.

HE SAID

"I plead the fifth."

BENEFIT

It's not cheating if you don't get caught.

DRAWBACK

He got caught. And named names.

HOW TO DEAL

Paper shredder. And clean up those e-mails.

11. Big Brother

THE BOSS

The tightfisted, sharp-eyed head honcho of corporate America, a.k.a. "the man."

DÉCOR

Security cameras.

HE SAID

"Loose lips sink ships."

BENEFIT

He always passes on the next wave of video camera glasses.

DRAWBACK

Make one personal photocopy and you're fired.

HOW TO DEAL

E-mail friends about how much you like working for him. He's reading them.

12. The Psychopath

THE BOSS

As brilliant as he is demented, he's just as likely to slash the company's budget as he is to riddle you with bullets.

HE SAID

"Oh, why is there plastic covering on the carpet? That's a good question. Please, come in and shut the door behind you."

INCIDENT

Nobody knows what happened to your predecessor.

BENEFIT

When he takes his lithium, he's actually quite pleasant.

DRAWBACK

You never know what's going to set him off.

HOW TO DEAL

Two words: body armor.

13. The Chair Chucker

THE BOSS

He has work to do, some *personal* work. A large man with a short temper, he sublimates his childhood trauma with a strong throwing arm. Top two chairs of choice: wooden hardback, metal folding. Now and then he'll toss in a stool or snow globe just to keep things fresh.

INCIDENT

He threw out his back picking up a recliner.

HE SAID

"Heads up!"

BENEFIT

Workman's comp.

DRAWBACK

Head trauma; bruises; at minimum, splinters.

HOW TO DEAL

Practice deep knee bends—good for ducking, dodging.

14. Talk to the Hand

THE BOSS

An out-of-touch thirtysomething, who only expresses herself through hackneyed cultural catchphrases.

SHE SAID

"Oh no you didn't!"

INCIDENT

She sprained her thumb during one of her "snaps."

BENEFIT

At least she's not a playa hata.

DRAWBACK

You can't decipher your performance review.

HOW TO DEAL

Don't even go there.

15. The Progressive

THE BOSS

She bikes to work, drinks free-trade coffee, smells like patchouli.

SHE SAID

"My body's nobody's body but mine."

INCIDENT

Tried to organize a hunger strike in support of the wrongfully imprisoned at Gitmo.

BENEFIT

She spends most of the workday canvassing inner-city districts for votes.

DRAWBACK

You have to circulate her petitions.

HOW TO DEAL

Donate a portion of your salary to liberal grassroots organizations in her name.

16. The Pimp

THE BOSS

A self-proclaimed man of the people, yet he offers no health insurance or overtime.

WARDROBE

Three-piece suits, fedora with peacock feather, bling.

HE SAID

"Where my money at?"

BENEFIT

Both manager and agent, he's out on the street mad hustling.

DRAWBACK

No personal days, and the hours are brutal.

HOW TO DEAL

Find a decent john who will get you off the street and make an honest woman of you.

17. By-the-Book Betty

THE BOSS

She can spot a fake expense a mile away.

SHE SAID

"Can you explain this $1,000 invoice from Harry's International House of Honeys?"

INCIDENT

Missing ink cartridges from office-supply closet triggered a company-wide lockdown.

BENEFIT

To mix things up a bit, she recently started ordering color paper clips.

DRAWBACK

Personal calls are deducted from your paycheck.

HOW TO DEAL

Keep your receipts. Credit card statements don't cut it.

18. The Jokester

THE BOSS

He's an equal-opportunity offender.

HE SAID

"Pull my finger."

INCIDENT

The fake bomb threat.

WARDROBE

Hand buzzer.

BENEFIT

The more you laugh, the bigger the raise.

DRAWBACK

Mandatory open-mic nights at the Peanut Gallery.

19. Wants to Be Your Buddy

THE BOSS

Big on high-fives and nicknames for his crew like "Big Guy" and "The Closer." Hangs out in your cubicle "just to shoot the shit."

INCIDENT

He showed up at your bachelor party.

WARDROBE

Buddy bands.

BENEFIT

Midday foosball tournaments. Free brewskis, too. But keep that on the D.L.

DRAWBACK

On the big Peterson account, he asked you to be his wingman.

HOW TO DEAL

Smile, nod, and take the free drinks. But do not, under any circumstances, give him your cell number. Ever.

20. The Letch

THE BOSS

Would rather discuss your cup size than your long-term growth projections.

INCIDENT

On your first day, he asked if your "girls" were team players, too.

HE SAID

"Nice tank top."

BENEFIT

If you got it, flaunt it.

DRAWBACK

He wants to be more hands-on.

HOW TO DEAL

Start wearing a burka.

21. The Whiz Kid

THE BOSS

You're old enough to be his father, but he makes more than your entire family combined.

DÉCOR

Movie posters. Lava lamps.

WARDROBE

Necktie, pinstripes, old-school red-and-black Jordans that are "sweet."

BENEFIT

Has to leave early to get home before six. Mom hates it when his dinner gets cold.

DRAWBACK

He scheduled the company Christmas party at the local arcade.

HOW TO DEAL

Buy a 30-pack for him and his underage friends.

22. The Micromanager

THE BOSS

In charge of half the department, she's an up-and-coming executive with her eyes on the corner office—and she's not about let you screw it up for her.

INCIDENT

When the deli ran out of chicken salad, you went ahead and ordered tuna salad for the staff lunch meeting without running it by her first. Mistake.

SHE SAID

"This report looks great. I'm just going to massage it a bit."

BENEFIT

No accountability.

DRAWBACK

Two years in, she still doesn't trust you to send out a fax.

HOW TO DEAL

CC her on everything.

23. Pregnant Boss

THE BOSS

Large and in charge, she's a simmering cauldron of unpredictable mood swings and unmitigated emotional outbursts.

INCIDENT

When you had to fill in for her husband at Lamaze class.

SHE SAID

Do you like Ariel or Sasha? Mica or Hannah? Cole or Rain? Oh, before you go, wanna touch my belly?

WARDROBE

The first two trimesters: sweatpants. The last trimester: muumuus.

BENEFIT

Maternity leave.

DRAWBACK

Take the last ice cream bar and she will kill you.

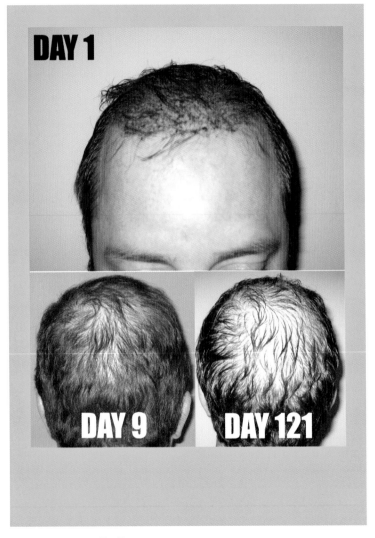

24. Balding Boss

THE BOSS

Hell hath no fury like a man naturally, prematurely, bare-headed.

HE SAID

"Bald is the new black."

INCIDENT

When the gels and goops failed, and after the hair plug catastrophe, you had to go rug shopping with him at Locks of Love.

BENEFIT

Instituted Hat Day Fridays.

DRAWBACK

What he lacks in hair, he more than makes up for in mis-directed rage.

HOW TO DEAL

Be a team player: Shave your head.

25. The Twelve-Stepper

THE BOSS

Fresh out of his most recent stint in rehab, he's back and better than ever. You, on the other hand, are still trying to recover emotionally from his last relapse.

HE SAID

"Hi, my name is Al and I'm an alcoholic, but that doesn't mean I can't party sober after work with you guys."

INCIDENT

Rock bottom.

BENEFIT

Step eight: Make amends.

DRAWBACK

He's burned so many bridges, you're his de facto sponsor.

HOW TO DEAL

The Serenity Prayer's not just for addicts anymore.

26. Mr. Hollywood

THE BOSS

He had two hits in the '80s and started his own production company. Now, he coasts on royalties and spends most of his day playing online poker.

CELL PHONE

He lunches at the Ivy, alone, working two cell phones at once, often calling himself.

HE SAID

"Here's my hot idea: a gross-out sex comedy set in high school. It's never been done!"

BENEFIT

You don't have to do any work because the only thing he's producing is videos from his Webcam.

DRAWBACK

You get paid when he gets paid. And it's mostly back-end.

HOW TO DEAL

Pretend you know what you're talking about, tell him he's great at his job, and short the stock in any company that produces his next film.

27. The Sleigh Driver

THE BOSS

His Royal Highness sits on his throne in the North Pole ordering elfin plebes to wrap this, whittle that, and get him a fresh beer. The gut isn't from candy alone: "North Pole Ale. Because It's Cold Up There."

INCIDENT

A saint? Hardly. Last Christmas, he eliminated collective bargaining and unilaterally renegotiated the minimum wage to one M&M an hour.

HE SAID

"Get me my sleigh, woman!"

BENEFIT

Recently, Mrs. Claus got tired of the "ho ho ho" joke and slept with the good-looking elf.

DRAWBACK

He knows when you are sleeping, he knows when you're awake, he knows damn well what goes on in his toy shack.

HOW TO DEAL

Sit on the foot of his throne and rub his feet.

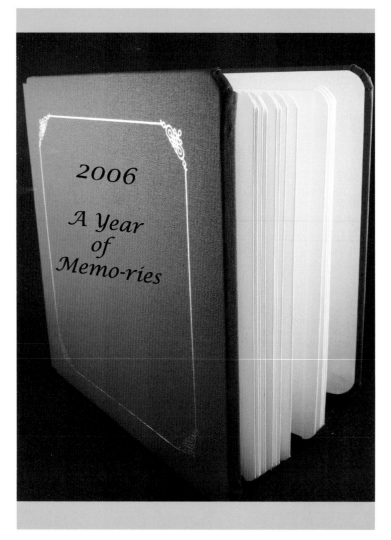

28. The Memo-ist

A firm believer in leaving a paper trail, this cataloger of corporate codes and regulations knows the ins and outs of the office. Please refer all questions or concerns to her, per her earlier memo.

In 2006, she turned a year's worth of memos into a suede-bound limited edition, giving it out as a Christmas gift to hundreds of employees at every branch in lieu of monetary bonuses. It is estimated the company heirloom cost over $75,000.

April 25, 2006: "New Fire Drill Procedure."
June 7, 2006: "Congrats to Sylvia James for 10 years of service. Way to go, Sylvia!"
Aug. 19, 2006: "We got the Riley account. Let's celebrate in the conference room in 10 minutes."
Nov. 11, 2006: Memo on how to compose memoranda.

Recycling is up 300 percent for the year.

Can never say you didn't get the memo.

Use the suede-bound book as a doorstop.

29. The Patriarch

THE BOSS

The same man who taught you and your siblings about the birds and the bees now signs off on your T&E's.

DÉCOR

Just like when you were a kid: Dad's is huge and has its own bathroom, your older brother's has a fridge, and you and your sister share a cubicle off the kitchen.

HE SAID

"Because I said so."

BENEFIT

The only work environment where "But Timmy does it all the time" is an appropriate counterargument.

DRAWBACK

If you thought sibling rivalry was bad around the dinner table, just wait until you go toe-to-toe with your sister in the boardroom.

HOW TO DEAL

Remember: Mom loves you all the same.

30. 30-Across

THE BOSS

A six-letter word for "knowledgeable showoff," this word freak demonstrates her mental superiority by leaving the daily crossword puzzle finished on her desk for all to see.

SHE SAID

"Oh, you do the Jumble. How cute."

INCIDENT

You found a number to a crossword help hotline in her Rolodex.

BENEFIT

While she's dashing off the morning puzzle, you can do a sudoku.

DRAWBACK

Not only does she make more money than you, she also has a better vocabulary, casually tossing out five-dollar words in meetings.

HOW TO DEAL

Take the twenty or so minutes she devotes every day to her beloved X-word to make overseas calls, gossip, shop online.

31. Recently Separated

THE BOSS

He has more time on his hands than he knows what to do with, so he works late and comes in on the weekends—and expects you to do the same.

DÉCOR

Suitcase, pullout couch, and a hot plate.

INCIDENT

On a work trip to Tokyo he asked to be dropped off at the red light district.

BENEFIT

Too busy discussing strategy with his divorce attorney to notice you take an extra half-hour for lunch.

DRAWBACK

Not only does he spend more time at the office, he started following you home after work, too.

HOW TO DEAL

Recommend a good marriage counselor.

32. Tenured

THE BOSS

The authority on nineteenth-century emerging economies, with an emphasis on the Reconstruction South, this bespectacled big man on campus runs his department with an iron fist (and a plethora of teaching assistants).

WARDROBE

Select items from Daffy's: Bargains for Millionaires.

INCIDENT

The footnotes imbroglio of 2004.

HE SAID

"Finished grading those midterms? Wonderful. Now you can get a jump on next semester's syllabus!"

BENEFIT

One word: sabbatical.

DRAWBACK

Within the ivy-covered walls of academia, he's considered a rock star; to the rest of the world, he's just another guy deep in thought, stroking his chin.

33. The Dilettante

THE BOSS

Unbelievably rich—his great-grandchildren's grandchildren won't have to work a day in their lives. But he still comes into the office 300 times a year just for kicks.

WARDROBE

The previous night's tuxedo.

HE SAID

"I really tied one on last night. I'm going to lie down for a yawn, so you take the wheel."

BENEFIT

Wants to be treated like the next guy . . .

DRAWBACK

. . . if the next guy were the United States ambassador to Papua New Guinea.

HOW TO DEAL

Hope he remembers you in his will.

34. The Misanthrope

THE BOSS

While some bosses discriminate against women, others men, she doesn't believe either sex is worth its salt.

DÉCOR

The collected works of Arthur Schopenhauer.

SHE SAID

"The more people I meet, the more I like my dog."

BENEFIT

Even when you screw up, you live up to her expectations.

DRAWBACK

Casual Fridays only exacerbate the situation.

HOW TO DEAL

Wear black, drink black coffee, turn to her side—the dark.

35. The Backstabber

THE BOSS

A former break buddy, he sold you out faster than you could say "annual review." He's now the head of your department.

INCIDENT

When his boss was out on maternity leave, he moved right into her office—and her accounts.

HE SAID

"It's not personal; it's just business."

BENEFIT

The sad truth is that he's not good at his job and you are. Sooner or later he will be exposed.

DRAWBACK

Until then, he will eliminate all those who know.

HOW TO DEAL

Turnabout is fair play: If he's always taking credit for your work, take a dive on a project.

36. The Junior Capitalist

THE BOSS

She's six years old, and no one's gonna tell her what to do on *her* side of the sidewalk.

INCIDENT

She was late to her shift because she couldn't find her roller skates.

SHE SAID

"You call that stirring? My little sister can stir better than that."

BENEFIT

She has cool stuff.

DRAWBACK

She won't let you play with it.

HOW TO DEAL

Tattle.

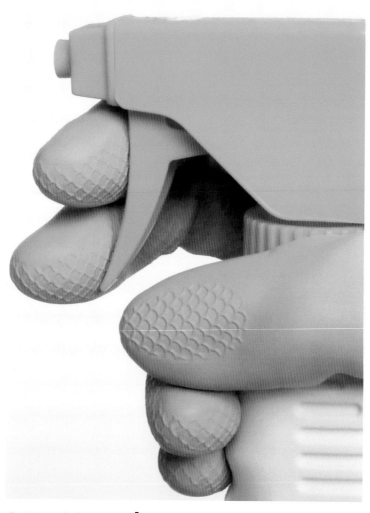

37. Mr. Clean

THE BOSS

A high-powered man with a cabinet full of high-powered cleansers. He scrutinizes your fourth-quarter projections as carefully as he does your nails for dirt.

DÉCOR

A large number of flat, shiny surfaces. His keyboard is dusted on the hour. And do not sit in his hypoallergenic chair; you take public transportation to work.

HE SAID

"Do you have any idea where that has been?"

BENEFIT

He smells pretty.

DRAWBACK

The surgical mask is a bit much for an investment consultant.

HOW TO DEAL

Rinse and repeat.

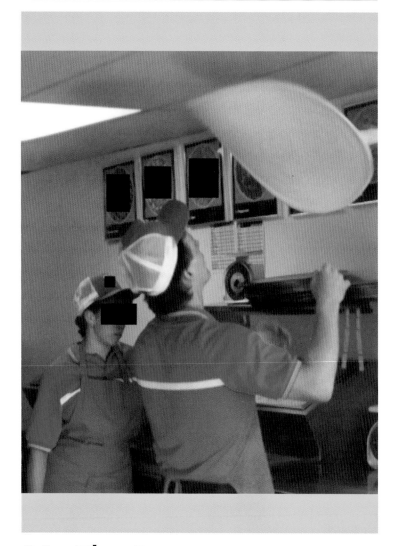

38. The Dropout

THE BOSS

He moved out at sixteen, spent his college fund (four summers detailing cars) on a sweet 944 Porsche he calls Sarah. Now, he's twenty-four and he manages his parlor and flips his pies with pride.

HE SAID

"When do you turn eighteen?"

INCIDENT

When you found his GED prep book.

BENEFIT

He motivates you to get good grades.

DRAWBACK

He asks about your sister.

HOW TO DEAL

If there's a problem, call his parents.

39. Pharaoh

THE BOSS

He's not much of a manager, but he can't exactly get fired.

INCIDENT

The time it rained frogs.

HE SAID

"Lazy, that's what you are, Moses—lazy! Now get to work. You will not be given any straw, yet you must produce your full quota of bricks." Exodus 13:5–6.

BENEFIT

Nice palace.

DRAWBACK

The whole "slavery" thing.

HOW TO DEAL

Stick it out until the Exodus.

40. Madame Secretary

THE BOSS

A thirty-year office veteran, she's made more copies than executive decisions.

DÉCOR

Pictures of her nieces, nephews, and cats.

WARDROBE

Pearls, so she says.

BENEFIT

The ten minutes of peace and quiet you get when she takes her hacking cough outside for the hourly secretary smoke break.

DRAWBACK

Parliament Menthol breath.

HOW TO DEAL

Send her roses on her birthday with a note, "From a secret admirer." That will keep her smiling for at least a few days.

41. Hot Boss (B.I.L.F.)

THE BOSS

She's three levels above you and way out of your league. She has every guy eating out of the palm of her hand; there is no task—no matter how trivial, inconvenient, or belittling—she can't get them to do.

WARDROBE

Tight button-down blouse, skirt, and legs that simply won't quit.

SHE SAID

"The Tokyo office is calling late tonight. You don't mind staying, do you, handsome?"

BENEFIT

Poolside meetings at the annual company retreat.

DRAWBACK

It's next to impossible to get any real work done while she's around.

HOW TO DEAL

Keep your head down and think about baseball.

42. The Blue Blood

THE BOSS

Born with a silver spoon in his mouth, he's stealing food off your plate by running the company into the ground.

WARDROBE

Seersucker suit, custom-made silk monogrammed shirt, saddle shoes.

INCIDENT

He liquidated the firm's pension plan to pay back investors on his failed Caribbean oil-drilling venture.

BENEFIT

Always shares when Mummy sends crumpets.

DRAWBACK

Your stock options aren't worth the paper they're printed on.

HOW TO DEAL

Get in touch with the Securities and Exchange Commission.

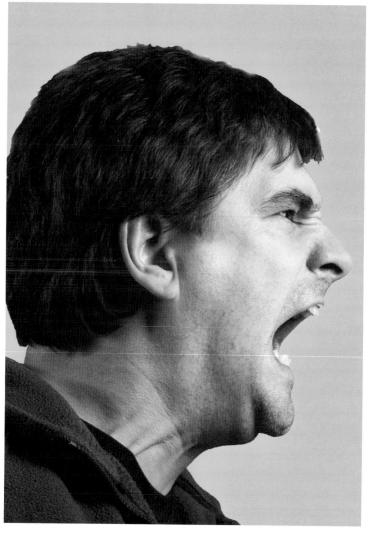

43. The Screamer

THE BOSS

Usually found on the city desk of large metropolitan news-papers, trading floors, or, in this case, a nondescript office complex outside of Peoria, Illinois, he's actually not that bad of an employer: he's competent, he lets you work on exciting projects, and he appreciates the work you do—until you screw up, when his temper flares and the decibel level rises.

INCIDENT

The same morning they installed stained-glass windows in reception, you misfiled the Wheeler report, then spent the rest of the afternoon combing rose-tinted silica out from the carpet fibers.

HE SAID

"I DON'T WANT TO HEAR ANY EXCUSES! JUST GET IT DONE!! DON'T MAKE ME START YELLING!!"

BENEFIT

He comes in loud and clear.

DRAWBACK

Tinnitus.

HOW TO DEAL

Earplugs.

44. Mr. Wonderful

THE BOSS

Charming, handsome, debonair, he's happily married with twin girls. He's also attentive, supportive, and sends you flowers on your birthday. Ladies, you'll lie down in front of a bus for him, even though he's paying you less than your male co-workers.

WARDROBE

Sadly, a wedding ring.

INCIDENT

You accepted his invitation to come by his house, and arrived just as he and his wife were on their way out for "date night." You spent the rest of the evening bottle-feeding his two colicky newborns.

BENEFIT

Doodling your hyphenated names together over and over on his personalized stationery almost makes the fantasy seem real. Almost.

DRAWBACK

His wife is prettier than you. Smarter, too.

HOW TO DEAL

Ask for a reassignment. Or stay and take out your sexual frustrations on the unpaid intern.

45. Mr. Five-Point Plan

THE BOSS

He's known exactly what he wants to do—and how to do it—since he was a kid instructing Dad precisely where to construct the moat and drawbridge around the sand castle. Once he sets a plan in motion, you can either get on board or get left behind at the station.

HE SAID

"First things first. Let's isolate the problem. Get it right in the crosshairs. After we've identified what's wrong, we brainstorm for solutions. Next, we set up a system so this type of thing never happens again. After our new platform is up and running, we should monitor it to make sure it's operating at 100 percent. Once in place, we can react seamlessly. Failure is not an option, gentlemen. Meeting adjourned."

INCIDENT

When his plan to streamline interoffice communication actually took six points, he was inconsolable.

BENEFIT

Your to-do list pretty much takes care of itself.

DRAWBACK

Maybe telemarketing doesn't really need such careful planning.

HOW TO DEAL

1. Arrange a meeting.
2. Highlight things that are going well between the two of you.
3. Discuss areas in which your relationship could still use some improvement.
4. Come to a mutual understanding about each other's goals.
5. Hand in your resignation.

46. The Infirm

THE BOSS

Perpetual runny nose, bloodshot eyes, swollen glands, hoarse voice. She doesn't take her sick days because she *always* gives her job 110 percent, and you, walking pneumonia.

WARDROBE

Germ-infested shawl she wraps around her chest, regardless of the season, and a box of tissues with aloe.

SHE SAID

(*Cough, cough*) "Finally, it's loosening up."

BENEFIT

The pseudoephedrine usually knocks her out for most of the afternoon.

DRAWBACK

She likes to work with you, side by side.

HOW TO DEAL

25,000 mg of vitamin C per day.

47. Out to Pasture

THE BOSS

He was once a mighty captain of industry, but the neurons aren't firing like they used to. He keeps showing up at the office, even though he hasn't had a new idea since the Roosevelt Administration. He's already worked through six "retirement" parties and, worst of all, still thinks he runs the place. Lucky for you, the powers that be made it your job to handle him, on top of everything else you have to do.

HE SAID

"Operator, give me Sycamore-4-3317."

INCIDENT

When he tried to make a phone call from the water fountain.

BENEFIT

He's like your grandfather.

DRAWBACK

Except your grandfather remembers who you are the day after you see him.

HOW TO DEAL

Give him a glass of warm milk, turn down the lights, and let him drift off to sleep.

48. The Fitness Fanatic

THE BOSS

Works hard, plays harder. This no-nonsense iron man knows just how to make the most of his lunch hour: 15 minutes lats, 15 minutes pecs, 15 minutes arms, 15 minutes glutes. And you're the lucky one who gets to spot him.

WARDROBE

Power suit in the morning, singlet at lunch.

HE SAID

"Feel the burn, baby!"

BENEFIT

The post-workout cooldown.

DRAWBACK

If he so much as sees a carb, he'll body-slam your ass against the filing cabinets.

HOW TO DEAL

Next workout, call him a girly man, hoping he'll try to break the club's bench press record. Maybe he'll pop a bicep.

ALAN ENDE
and "REGGIE"

49. The Ventriloquist

THE BOSS

Total control freak. Won't let me do anything on my own. He's always putting words in my mouth, has his hands all over me, makes me sit on his lap. And after a show, do we go out for a beer? No. He just says good night and locks me in a box.

HE SAID

"So Reggie, what do you want to do? What's that? You want to sing some Sinatra? 'My Way'? Now you're talkin'!"

PAY

So far I haven't seen dime one. He assures me the dough will roll in when Broadway starts looking for the next *Avenue Q*. Until then, hand to mouth—*his* hand to *my* mouth.

BENEFIT

The man does give quite the back massage.

DRAWBACK

He calls me dummy. What's this, the Dark Ages? The term for my people is Wooden American.

HOW TO DEAL

Give him the silent treatment and watch the audience heckle.

50. '70s Dude Turned Corporate

THE BOSS

By wearing his hair a little long and keeping an electric guitar in his lap, he tries to convince his junior employees that he's cool, and a cool boss is a cool guy to work for. But cool is *not* repeatedly killing your work, throwing his head back in helplessness, and saying, "Dudes, we are screwed. Come in with brilliant ideas tomorrow"—insert guitar riff—"or we're going lose this account."

DÉCOR

Trippy, psychedelic Grateful Dead concert posters with pictures of tiny, pink, naked ladies falling through an hourglass. If he likes you, he'll put on the black light for you.

INCIDENT

During staff meetings he plays air guitar.

BENEFIT

You have much better odds of getting work approved if you know your Dylan. It's basically a game of name that tune. If you can get "All Along the Watchtower" in three chords, you're golden.

DRAWBACK

He's won every major award in his field—the trophies surround him like an audience cheering him on and intimidating you.

HOW TO DEAL

Learn "Stairway."

51. Your Boss

THE BOSS

WARDROBE

DÉCOR

BENEFIT

DRAWBACK

HOW TO DEAL

PHOTOGRAPHERS

The Former Thespian: istockphoto/Mark Stout
The Big-Game Hunter: Peter Lynn, ISF/Robert Lerich
The Napoleon: istockphoto/Vasko Miokovic Photography
The Veteran: istockphoto/Joshua Sowin
The Former All-American: istockphoto/Wolfgang Lienbacher
The Made Man: istockphoto/Duncan Walker
First Position of Power: istockphoto/Avid Creative, Inc.
The Heir Apparent: David Berman
The M.B.A.: istockphoto/Luis Alvarez
Chief Elusive Officer: istockphoto/Timothy Large
Big Brother: istockphoto/Andres Rodriguez
The Psychopath: istockphoto/Andrew_Howe
The Chair Chucker: istockphoto/Jan Gottwald, Ben Goode
Talk to the Hand: istockphoto/sdominick
The Progressive: Michelle Malkin
The Pimp: istockphoto/upheaval
By-the-Book Betty: istockphoto/digital bristles
The Jokester: dreamstime/Adinan
Wants to Be Your Buddy: istockphoto/studiovancaspel
The Letch: istockphoto/Desktop Studio
The Whiz Kid: dreamstime/Dannyphoto80
The Micromanager: istockphoto/xploresoft, LLC
Pregnant Boss: dreamstime.com/Andrew Taylor
Balding Boss: courtesy of Seth Garon (battleagainstbald.com)
The Twelve-Stepper: istockphoto/Simone Van Den Berg
Mr. Hollywood: istockphoto/studiovancaspel
The Sleigh Driver: Wayne Whaley, Curtis Palmer
The Memo-ist: istockphoto/Craig Veltri
The Patriarch: Rebeca Lai, istockphoto/duncan1890
30-Across: istockphoto/Melissa Schwartz
Recently Separated: istockphoto/Karen Struthers
Tenured: istockphoto/Lisegagne.com
The Dilettante: istockphoto/Dennis Steininger
The Misanthrope: istockphoto/smitea
The Backstabber: istockphoto/digitalefx.ca
The Junior Capitalist: Clayton Esterson & Podlich
Mr. Clean: dreamstime/Lori Sparkia
The Dropout: Ray Conrado
Pharaoh: istockphoto/ratsuben
Madame Secretary: David Berman
Hot Boss (B.I.L.F.): dreamstime/Tadija Majstorovic

The Blue Blood: istockphoto/Robert Young
The Screamer: istockphoto/imbarney22
Mr. Wonderful: dreamstime/Dewayne Flowers
Mr. Five-Point Plan: dreamstime/Andresr
The Infirm: istockphoto/Wouter van Caspel
Out to Pasture: dreamstime/Raymond Truelove
The Fitness Fanatic: istockphoto/Lucian Coman
The Ventriloquist: Courtesy of Alan Ende
'70s Dude Turned Corporate: Roland Tanglao
Contributing photographer: Jo Ann Snover

THE PHOTOGRAPHED

The Pimp: Jeremiah Deasey
The Made Man: Duncan Walker
Madame Secretary: Denise Ortell, Meghan O'Neill
Recently Separated: Andrew Howe
The Junior Capitalist: Clare Lawless, Grace Lawless
The Heir Apparent: Rob Seitelman
Balding Boss: Seth Garon (battleagainstbald.com)
The Ventriloquist: Alan Ende and Reggie
'70s Dude Turned Corporate: Derek Miller

All images used in this publication are for illustrative purposes only, and all persons included in the imagery are models rather than the actual persons depicted.

WRITING CREDITS

Miles Doyle, Ben Adams, and Betsy Lerner, who added the intelligent humor
Dan Berman: The Jokester, Recently Separated, Wants to Be Your Buddy
Lori Segal: Pregnant Boss, The Patriarch, Too Much Info (cut)
Christine Liu: Tenured, Commander in Chief (cut)
Jessica Dixon: Symphony Conductor (cut)
Robert M. Errera: Former Thespian
Connor McClure: Lowly Celebrity Magazine Editor (cut)

Thank you so much Alec Brownstein, Greg Racz, and Ellen Racz for pointing out the crap and polishing the turds.

Publicists: Yelena Gitlin, Wendy Morris, and Katie Rosin of Kampfire Films.

Amazing interns: Christine Liu, Lindsay Eisenstadt, Eric Simmons, Jessica Dixon, Jason Working, Molly Kordares, Sarah Peavey, Kate Paulin, Connor McClure

ACKNOWLEDGMENTS

These books wouldn't be here, or very good, without my brilliant and patient editor Miles Doyle; my superagent Betsy Lerner of Dunow, Carlson & Lerner Agency; the cover and interior design by Elizabeth Van Itallie; the illustrations by Laurel Tyndale; or Karen Rinaldi, Bloomsbury USA's publisher, for her unwavering commitment to schadenfreude.

Thanks to: Elisa Resnick, Rachel Resnick, Jackie Resnick and Clown Resnick, Kristina Marchitto, Jeff Moores, Courtney Thompson, Dylan Lynch, Tony Larson, Shara Mendelsohn, Lucia Martinez Martinez, Rebecca Farber, Ali Brafman, Laura Torchin, Alec Brownstein, Chris Nichols, Lori Muslow, Chesley, Stu, Katie Claypoole, Nate Taylor as always, Simply Hired's Phil Carpenter and former Kay Luo, Alex Finkelstein, Broken Cup coffee bar's Bob and Bruce, Allan Shapiro, Julie Soefer, Jennifer Caldwell, Mary Tucker, Rob Seitelman, Barrie Gordon, Barnes and Noble's Frank Hoffman and Jeff McLaughlin, K. C. Gentzel, Laura Mazzullo, Mareen Fischinger, Brian Gadinsky, Scot Candioti, Zack Hirsch, The Apostolati (Nicholas, Andreas, Danielle, Mom and Dad), Julie Rappaport, Jesse Resnik, Joe Narciso, Lynn Weinerman, Claire C. Yaptangco at Vault.com, Laura Mazzullo, Shari Gersch, Sandy Cullinin, Jan (Fossil Freak, Flickr), Catherine Herrick, Judith and Mort Gerberg, the Mascolos, Nancy Lainer, the D'Agostinos, Greg Racz, Alexa Jervis, Daniel Racz, Ellen Racz, Graham Balch, Victoria Roberts, William Noto, Chinkara Singh, Chris and Amy Nichols, Craig and Heather Stouffer, Ben Coplon, Kristina Justh, Eric Van Skyhawk, Lara Wagner, Alison Molstre, Chantel Nash, Laura Torchin, Denise Lawless, Christian Aeschliman, Jill Golden, Scott Mitnick, Kim Mitnick, Jason and Whitney Tandon, Cynthia Stewart, Dolores Sparks, Wallis Post, Deborah Lester of Perry Street Cakes, Lisa Timmons, Joe Dubin, Katie Green, Shelby Reynolds, Josh and Chris Cahill, Owen and Courtney DeHoff, Jeff Nussbaum, Michael Corkery, Chris and Lorna Sharp, Natalie Tripp, Jimmy Yao, Dr. Deborah Bernbaum, Paul Siegel, Jessica Smollins, Michael Wyszomierski, Jim & Mahalie Pech, Ping Ping, Elijah van der Giessen, Kai Pradel, Kimberly Holden, Jess Barron, Beata Wojciechowska, Denny Jones, Jeannette Balleza at Deadfred.com, Paul Downey. I apologize if I miscredited anyone, didn't attribute proper credit, or misspelled anyone's name.

Ann Sanfedele took the photograph that illustrated "Your Last Day," in *50 Days Worse Than Yours*. Her name was misspelled. home.nyc.rr.com/annsansdirectory/